Patchwork

by

Dorothy Devine

Fifty Years of Poetry

Chair Yoga, Circle of Life, Fatigue, Letting Go, Headstrong, and *What Changes?* previously appeared in the Fourth Annual Anthology, Neighborhood Guild Creative Writers (2017)

Four Haiku for Fall, Halloween, Horoscope, Oak Moon, Sonnet to My Love, Starting Over A-Z, The Best Things in Life Are Still Free, Veterans Day, and *Violence for Peace?* previously appeared in the Third Annual Anthology, Neighborhood Guild Creative Writers (2016)

Violence for Peace? was part of a Poets Speaking Up program in March 2016. *Solo Song for Kay Boyle* is inspired by Ms. Boyle's 1922 poem, *Monody to the Sound of Zithers.*

ISBN # 9781092379243

First edition: April 2019

Patchwork

by

Dorothy Devine

To Holly Fuscaldo
with gratitude —

Dorothy Devine

To Bea

Souvenirs

souvenirs – that's all I have to show for it
a kid's smiling 5-year old portrait
poles for a teepee now rotted
jeans patched with hippie embroidery
     a small N.L.F. flag.

oh, and a few beads
a box with your writing calling me "starshine"
a Gay Revolution pin – lavender star, red letters
stash boxes and pipes
     souvenirs.

rings of silver, turquoise, scrimshaw
chained and carved and hammered
     (like my heart)
one of gold, the narrowest at the jewelers
a marriage so understated, gone so long ago
rings of love and failure
     now I keep them in a box.

I sleep alone now mostly or
rather with Isis, a cat who'd
rather sleep on me
than anywhere
I still like skinny-dipping
I still move every year or so
     yet not so far.

I'm in the middle of my Saturn cycle
heavy Piscean influences wash over me
I watch the moon changes in stark concentration
I'm waiting it out
     looking at my souvenirs.

Dream

I am
floating
in a warm bluegreen
sea
wrapped in soft
seaweed

and mermaids
and women
float around
their arms are
gentle
like the tides

their kisses
never
insist

it all flows
flows

Starshine Poem

within
you are starshine
clarity
coolness and
space

multiple versions
vanish
it is here
I want to know

to touch
with that which
inside me,
is also Truth

Violence for Peace?

Was it the daughter of the labor lawyer
Or the dark-haired woman from the Midwest
Who came to our apartment in Somerville
To dare us to go to war against our country?
Such crazy times, we tried to teach peace.

Summer workshops in the suburbs
About the war in Vietnam.
Block by block, more homes opened
All sorts of families talking, reading
Kind people, parents of soldiers cared.

At school, study groups on race and poverty
Women's rights, the labor movement,
How war and peace were decided
We loved our country, wanted it to be
Just, helpful, and fair.

She sat, legs spread, in high boots, tight jeans,
Before young (mostly) men of Boston's New Left
Sexual pose deliberate; speaking just to the men
Are you men enough to attack your country?
Are your balls as big as mine?

The United States was more violent
Rocks were thrown, windows smashed,
Buildings were bombed, protestors shot
My car was torched – I left, used a new name
Avoided my old collective's trials.

The dark-haired woman in and out of jail for
riots and disturbances,
The lawyer's daughter charged with murder for
driving a getaway car
Years passed – one learned family law, nominated
as a judge
The other a professor at the very school
She once shut down.

I stayed at last in a town with "peace" in its name
Finally let love grow
Advocated for our river's health
Planned bike and walking trails
Had modest jobs, work with elders, cancer patients.

I never hit or shot anyone (in this way I was true to
myself),
Rocks were thrown at me, I never broke a window
But I was angry, as angry as those insolent women
Flirting, cursing, dancing to war, while I
Drifted alone, dreaming of peace.

Safe

Jean Tingeley designs
sculpture-machines that
self-
destruct

is marriage
a
machine?

my husband,
my husband –
repeating an enormity
I have
failed
to grasp

a huge
solidity
I called
it once

I thought I
would
always
be safe

I was the simpleton

Free Road

The roads were full of energy
Bright and wild, alive
Long-haired men, girls peasant-dressed
I ask my soon-to-be fiancé
To leave his car behind

He and I stand on the highway
Smile, raise our thumbs
I need to be happening
Soon I take this to excess
So restless, confused why

Sleep under tarps and driftwood
Drivers get us high
With damp sand in tender places
Meet a pair headed to an inn
Leave the free road behind

Stay where we can take a shower
Talk about our Eastern schools
As summer-break college students
Have a good meal, good wine
Predicted lives again

It took me years to remember how
Desperate I was to break free
It took me just as many years
To understand those choices carried
Some stunning sorts of loss

New Year's Resolution 1971

1. don't fall in love.

        don't sense the pull of dark
energy center

        don't covet tight muscled arm
skin

        or search gone eyes

1. don't fall in love.

Nickname: "Symphony"

Marriage gone, I was raised to feel
Devastated, lost
Here we are sitting with our feet
Hanging into the Grand Canyon

Your dark good looks
Captivate my eyes
We talk for hours
I learn so much from you

Things I haven't considered
Anarchy, gay revolution, your belief
Monogamy just can't work
Another heavy Scorpio in my life

Your nasal voice strident
Plays against exotic looks
We talk talk talk
I get a sunburn

Haight-Ashbury: we split in anger
Still never having touched
That last night you say you are cold
I don't know how to make you warm

For years my tries with women
Don't work better than married life
I only find you once again
In all my travels West

A decade later, I have no idea
Where you or your daughter might be
Changing sister/witch spirit
May your own bright dance make you warm

9

Horoscope

You are usually happier when you are taking chances, and
the best part is that they never run out. The more chances
you take the more you get.
 -- Holiday Mathis, **Providence Journal, 3-8-14**

Happier? But she was never happy
Over and over she thought, I do not belong here.
The chance she took was breaking away.

Superior on tests, privileged college student,
Child whose accomplishments should telegraph
That her parents did all right, after all.

Forget his Iwo Jima shell shock,
Her Paris-writer ambitions trapped in
suburbia,
Leave behind his fury and her Valium.

Education and poise should be a passport,
Yet she broke away from marriage
With no plan but California with a friend.

The predictable contained her, the unknown
beckoned,
She must move on from commune and
farmhouse
From mountains and from opposite coasts.

One bright dawn found her hitchhiking toward
Yosemite,
With a drifting daughter of Main Line Philadelphia
Two large trucks offered them rides.

As always, they climbed in to ride together,
But the truckers wanted them separate, exposed
We're getting out, she said.

Her companion made it to the roadside,
She felt a boot against her back, shot through
the air
Landed flat on her face, breathless.

She poured water over her hands from a
canteen,
Leaned on a tree, picked out gravel with a
pocket-knife.
Wondering this time, where *will* I belong?

February Poem

bad month
he slept with another
4 years ago
I sat on a cold stone bench
startled how little I cared

the next February we'd
just gotten married
don't know why I
know I was pushed by
my parents
       (we pledged ourselves to the
        world-wide struggle for freedom
        and justice)
           but
at least their daughter
wasn't
'ruined'

The next February I
came back from Cuba
pay toilets after
2 and a half months (a long time)
feeling needed and strong
everything free, work to do –
pay toilets, police again
and a tall stranger I am
supposed to touch
       (another had seemed
          like freedom)
and therefore leave

today
this February second
for some reason I'm not in California
my mother knows only a false address
I search (unsuccessfully four weeks)
for an apartment available for someone
who
        looks wild
              (as I must)

I nag a woman lover
the last man I lived with
(bright star)
chases his spirit to India
without coming by
        to say
              goodbye

I come into the kitchen
wash dishes left by others
and don't remember to eat
it's cold outside
I know I am adrift but
        don't know
              where to land

March will be a beautiful windy month
        of long walks
              alone outside.

Attica Massacre

today
>
> hangover tired at work
> messing up the keypunching
> thinking few thoughts

one thought
> "Stanley Bond Lives"

flashes
>
> cross uptight office scene
> white wall imagined with
> red-dripping words
> "Stanley Bond Lives"

last night's blues band drug-fueled games
> "Stanley Bond Lives"

people in the streets
> what of his tactics then?

today you feel like my brother

drawing mustaches on models
> from the *Bazaar* taken from
> a neighbor's mail
> "Stanley Bond Lives"

Clear

clear day
clear head
      I flow through life
      life flows through
           veins, heart, brain

bubbles
peacefully
      toward fingertips, hair-endings
      the muscles of my calves

life
love
      sunshine and clean air

Younger Moment

slim strawberry body
    full lower lip
        small high breasts of
        your nineteen years

    soft ass
    small hands

lying with you is like swimming
    the sidestroke to paradise
        free and high and easy
        a friend holding me firmly

    with smiles

Hippie Days

We loved Dr. Bronner's Soap
Because it felt good on our privates,
As we had so much sex.

When all the granola
Meant we sat on the john a long time,
Read his label rantings.

We hitchhiked happily
Mass. Ave. alone; and with a friend,
To New Hampshire, Chicago.

I alone to the Cape
Stayed with a National Lampoon guy,
Later a suicide – I'm here.

I try to catch in words
How we thought we were a family,
Thought that changed the world.

Forty-eight years later
My rantings (not Dr. Bronner's)
Are condensed.

Final Suitor

It was dangerous
To meet a man so transformative
More compelling
Than her mate, awakening
Daring for risk.

Two years later she's
Slid to a commune: tousled girls
Long-haired boys
"Gay Revolution" poster
Odor of herb.

When he returns, she
Shies from connection
She's entangled in
Ensemble recklessness
And so, he leaves.

As anti-drug as
One who counsels
Other war vets
Can be, he censures
Her liberties.

Striding away
He and dog named after
Vietnam scout dog depart
Strong sunlit duo,
Forever gone.

Going and Coming

I am afraid that loving me
is hurting you
you can have your own parties
        and travels and boys and joys
no need to help me hide out and lick
        my old wounds
so I keep going away

when my need brings me back
I find you stronger and more beautiful
        on each return
and when on this return you turn to me angry
(but it's funny how your anger seems
        just-like-love)
and say, "it mainly hurts me that
        you are afraid…"

I believe you.

Married Woman

Venus and Diana walked the forest of Olympus
speaking of trees and medicines and timeless ages
past
a bench in a clearing:
Aphrodite's daughters tumbled at her feet
the dog chased the milch goat
all about fecund: life and mothering
the clear power in woman
so awesome and so good

the huntress laced her sandals
for a run in the forest
come! sister deer! brother bug! –
a different kind of energy, power in motion –

yet as our clear eyes met, I thought,
how sweet it would be to be a tree in your forest
dance toward the moon –
as blessed as your babies:
plants, animals, children
as they grow!

Handshake

you somersaulted into the room
singing of love
that first time we met

and my mind thought
"yes"

when you had taken me up
on that thought
blooming nipples, taut body –

I got up to leave –
you shook
my hand

Starting Over: A - Z

Always starting over
But never finishing
Cursed with just enough money to get a ticket out
Determined to be self-defined
Expecting others to understand

For years you did not see the selfishness
Going out the door when things got hard
Heading west, or east, or north
Inventing reasons or chasing a crush
Just leaving loving friends behind

Keep away important questions
Like how to support yourself
Now and over the years
Or what sort of work could you do well
Perhaps to bring justice or peace

Questing, seeking, traveling a path,
Road, train line, hippie bus, hitching a ride
South of Eureka, California on a ranch
Transferred and "deeded to God"
Untouched by building codes and health laws

Vacant-minded and hidden in the woods
Waiting for a top-hatted drummer who could not
find her way
"X" means an unknown quantity
You remained a mystery far too long
Zealously you guarded hurt and blocked growth

Attic

it's these crazy dreams
again
about what love is
when love just is…

for we spend a dozen nights
speechless and sweating
on a mattress in an attic
with a balcony and magic

and then I left

Goodbye

I'm an expert at turning and running at airports
At sneaking out before people wake up
Wistfully eyeing sleeping forms

Telling folks I'll see them once more
Before they go or I go
And then dropping out of sight

This time is no different
I move my cartons
A painful all-day process

We have promised each other
We'll never live together again
I tell myself I have a few more things to pick up

But I shy away from that final hug
As if it might kill me
And I don't come back again

I never could say goodbye

Pain

pain: far from senseless, has its purpose
helps us to know we exist
we feel
we care
we identify our edges (the raw ones)

enough generalities: the pain I feel
to not have you
to not be near you –

tells me: that I can love
that I can care
that I can feel –
separates my identity from all
those other molecules

tells me, yes, I am alive

Chant

walking down the street alone
my footsteps chant your name
after all this time
but then: time is nothing.

all the tight frustration
an unmatched love that could have been
if you hadn't been under all that sedation
if I hadn't been rambling, jobless

if I had by then outgrown
begging for love
as if it was something I needed to take
as if I had nothing at all to give

all that historic passion
contained, still contained
and, in spite of all my changes
the ways I tell myself I love myself –

your name comes often
taunting, taunting
that unreasonable love a stopper in my heart
my bubbling, sparkling heart

a glass of rare champagne
to share with giggles
but that god-damn cork
just won't pop
out

Enticed

I thought with us it was just a question of
the right magical moment
alone

but when I take you to bed and start to
touch
you

you say
"you're so wild. you have to have time
and trust"

I say
"there are no walls between us but I want
to know all there is to know
of you"

but then coyly
I turn my back
hoping the curve of my hip
(should all else fail)
might entice you

Your Name Means 'Beautiful'

We share a crash pad, a commune
Laugh and dope in night streets, mimic Janis
Love is an adventure, not to find a mate
Won't ensnare us as it did our moms
Shoulder-by-shoulder, we stay safe.

I'm away: mostly to the Coast
Away in my mind, trying on girlfriends
Yet coach at your shoulder as, red-faced
You push your small unsullied daughter
Into this uncertain world.

First joined near Lizzie Borden's house
You stroked my legs with your long heavy hair
You were 'home' half a decade; another passed
Till I stopped dreaming my head on your shoulder
My truest safety under that hair.

You came for me just once, many more times
I returned to you, until you needed
To primal-scream me far away from your heart
I bounce your dimpled daughter on my shoulders
One more time, and then I travel on.

Stillness

we women, it seems
really don't understand
ourselves
or one another

or perhaps we just
focus too much energy
into interesting complexities
and habitual worry

but we should keep in mind:
a nervous woman can relax
in yielding to a touch,
a gentle stroke up tensing thigh

a chattering woman
sometimes needs a kiss
to halt onrushing attachment,
concern and words

sometimes a woman
wants to simply feel
letting you touch is a gift
deserving praise

a special thing
beyond all need
to touch
back

sometimes it is worse
to ask the reasons for her sadness,
sorrow is no lighter for
having been inadequately explained

sometimes it is best
to distract the worried
to clear the emotional and mental and verbal
with the direct and physical

reach for her:
touch
let the warmth spread
from body to body

the fire and the melting
the yielding
and the
taking

the noises
and
then
the quiet

stillness: the path there is
always a possibility
always just
one move away

Beware the Rescuer

When you're really down and out
Sitting in parks or on library steps
In a town that has never been good for you
Waiting for another day to end
Beware the rescuer.

Give yourself time to rise up
Find a good, safe place, work an extra job
Listen to your yoga teacher, not to drinkers
Consider new possibilities
Beware the rescuer.

At 28, you have never lived alone
Don't assume you need a coupled home
You need to discover your honorable work
Your own voice for change
Beware the rescuer.

For when you find love is gone
There will be nowhere to go, lots to lose
When you know you've written a good speech
But allowed her to give it
Beware the rescuer.

Go, sleep in your car one night
Realize who you are and who you have been
Know she will not tell you the truth:
That she has already found
A fresher fool to rescue.

Sexual Revolution

In the seventies, the saying
Was "Make Love Not War"
Every date ended with
The possibility of sex
You could sleep with the girl
You loved so deeply in high school
If you let her husband in

In Washington for a peace march
Group-grope where we stayed
We thought they would not
Let us share a room, eyes now wide
Authors, filmmakers played
There is a Pentagon "fuck-in"
Instead of a sit-in, we refrain

The wife who paid for her husband's
Grad school working in the courts
Holding off on children
Must convince doctors she is crazy
To gain permission to abort
It was too late when she saw
Buxom radical his new sport

One-night stands could yield life stories
Truthfully shared, yet
Never meet again
Marijuana-fueled behavior
Feels good with nothing left to say
Later we believe this
Helped derail much broader change

Pitfalls: solitude, infection
A man vowing he is gentle
Wakes me with his hands around my throat
You sleep with someone your best friend craved
Lose the important one, the friend
You fall in love, offer your heart
Find no way to grow from a casual start

These years bring soul exhaustion
Illness, pregnancy add new weight
Men-loving men now die
Women-loving-women want wives
Some give up their babies
Some die sick, ashamed, alone

Vermont

Twice tried life in the Green Mountains
Search for safety "back to the land"
Unfortunately, I bring myself along
Drama begets desertion
Hunters shoot deer in the yard
Mistake to move there in the Fall

No garden, chickens stop laying
Roads long white snow tunnels
Snowmobilers destroy quiet
Feed my college papers to the woodstove
Chase a musician to San Francisco
Dream new freedoms there

Change when I return in Spring
Household scattered, no way home
Blunder on my lonely birthday
Momentous nonchalant mistake
Instead of healing, one more wound
Alters the balance of my life

Several years later it is summer
Home a teepee I work alone to sew
Stay in the woods near old friends
Take cold baths in Crystal Lake
Regrettably, I invite someone along
Sidestep solo healing yet again

In a few years decisively pushed
Tired enough to slow my pace
See confusion made me callous
Broader devotion ousts my foolish ways
Now I live and learn alone
Mature at last beside the bay

Elusive

love
(ever elusive)
is the dream
on which we hang
our illusions

and sometimes
for all the trying
what is best effortless
and clearest free
slips away from our
(neurotic)
scrutiny

tests and measures
repelling pleasures
limits and possession
stifling expression
clinging stilling singing

and so in the end
I know more
of what love is
not
than what it be

it is not
unquestioning loyalty
nor proof of success
or happiness
nor is it genital
in the sense of
fidelity
or activity

those who act in love
before others
are often not
and those who do not act
so
often are

angry woman in a café:
"Love," she says coldly,
"is a game for children,"
but no,
it's not
that,
either

Point Zero

unknown and alone again
freedom in a different sense
back to point zero
the month's beginning

only the nights, the flow
of stars and the
fullness of the moon
will show this month's fruit

see how unknown and alone
will change
point zero...one...two...three
and each month around again
with a different lesson

month after month
on and on
year after year
if I don't learn my lesson
you'll show me again
and again until
I do

month after month
year after year
again and again

point zero…
incognito…
solo…

unknown and alone
again…
anything is possible

My Own Desert

certain migrations must be
completed
before the Hopi
return to
the Center of the Universe

coast to coast and
pole to pole
following the stars and
signs that each time it's
time to leave

to settle at long last in the
desert
for it is most difficult
they must remain pure
and pray for rain

thus must I learn the
lessons of my
migrations
follow the signs when it's
time to leave

returning at long last
to the hardening and craggy
mesa of myself
the knowledge of my own
hardness and clarities

singing and dancing
prayers
of gratitude and
celebration that

here in this
deserted and difficult
mesa
shall I find and praise
all I shall need

My Friend

We met at a party for Shakespeare's sister Joan
Who never wrote, never had a room of her own
I knew two guests; one played a drum
The short pretty blonde soon to break up with me
Must have been there, but I can't recall.

When I sat down on the stairs
By the soft pale woman with long red hair
A huge peace came over me, "I know you"
Six months later life's fated changes brought me
To settle in your village; we met to share poems.

For 30 years we circled at home and forest hearths
Celebrating solstices, equinoxes, neo-pagan dreams
Peace, survival for Mother Earth, all her creatures
Now we move as quiet wise-women
Subtly among more open beliefs in our town.

You helped me home from a date with my now wife
I was stranded as she bolted back to her boyfriend
I fear your flights in your husband's antique plane
Rejoice you are still safe when it is sold
We crave calm, safety, power to choose words well.

When cancer first surfaced I said I loved you
And you told me you loved me too
Not wanting you left here without my friendship
I sensed you hoped I would not, too
It's common for us to know but not say this.

You write in a closet in a home stuffed with books
You mourned my author mother, too
You have 12 books: poetry, science fiction/fantasy
Now a crime series with a supernatural side
World-rescuing shape-shifters with tiger eyes.

I pray for your fame: best-seller, movie deal
Enough money to live in Paris, do what you want.
Now your long hair is frosted with white
We talk of cats, dogs, departed parents, work, health
Yearnings, children, step-children, spouses, hopes.

If you wrote it, your childhood would test belief
Much more than my twenties vagrant wandering
We will meet until, for some reason, we cannot
Most of all, we offer each other courage
You are my best friend.

Black and White

Leaving black and white for color
Like Pleasantville or Dorothy in Oz,
I must go, but still feel abashed
After all the conflict with my parents
He and I did not win, I lost

A classmate also leaves her husband
Despite Givenchy wedding gown
Travels to Findhorn's spiritual lights
With my dwindling resources
It's bright riffraff, Cambridge-Boston nights

Temping in a Harvard office
My first-ever love comes in,
I pretend I do not see him
Sighted or blind, my heart writhes
Slashed to zero as fire will go to ash

Finally lose those mismatched lovers
Who savored a vagabond stance,
Feel blue-green of our Mother Earth
Cradling you, him, her, me – all
Join others to worship and celebrate Her

It's a miracle I am here
Men I knew then are not alive
It took a decade to get home
Do work best done alone
Put myself first, be calm, survive

Quite some time to find a focus
Old friends became rare booksellers
Consultants, blue jean merchants
Disney artists, tarot readers, moms
Wives and nurses, storytellers

It's a process full of twists and turns
As I begin to feel I'm good
Choose a good town, make a small home
Work to keep it safe, secure
Treasure new and old friends, write some poems

The Will of the Trees

As we walk by the sand pit
I'm wearing your ancient
    straw hat with the
    sky painted under the
    rim
"People shoot guns in here,"
you say, but
we walk on.

Viewing the huge gouge in our Mother
"No wonder the Indians are angry"
and we speak of a native leader's spirit quest
his journey to live on the
land after a lifetime of organizing
which somehow
gives me hope.

On to
the second sandpit
older, filled
with foliage
teetering on your clogs
on the rock pile pathway
discovering here a huge frog
a lifetime of rushes and small birds
skimming water
and even trees
begin to return.

"The trees are causing
what's happening in the world today"
you share
"They want the earth back for
themselves, for they are much better
to Her."

I take
all the clear high energy
of our meeting
and focus it
on this
abundant
reforestation.

Artful

Statuesque, similarly schooled
You have rainbow cigarette papers
I am your matron of honor in a vintage dress
As godmother to your daughter
Show another lifestyle choice

The arts center job you get me
Brings concerts, art shows, dance
Life changes, I find my way
That work lasts just a year, yet
I am never without work again

We often talk of love and health
Responsibilities of only-daughters' lives
Watch our fathers, then our mothers die
Share care choices, final rites
Discuss sound use for family wealth

You work a potter's wheel, make paper
Use leaves and feathers to print
Your daughter dies and you create
A brightly-painted children's book
And here I find her – here she still lives

You work for good, never for profit
For literacy, community, art in schools
Your solar power, gardens, compost,
Chickens – part of a city's rebirth
You're still dancing with joints rebuilt

The photographs and trinkets
Of old New England family down to one
Become assemblages, collages
Of bygone lives you thus release
Without an heir, you use them to create

We age, we work to gain detachment
Tragedy, suffering part of human life
Grief does not destroy you, but suggests
One more way for you to teach
Yet again, your words bring me peace

Listening

thanks to you for
listening
to my self-indulgences
not with lazy disinterest
but
with gentle distress
caring for me
anyway

you understand
that my changes
scare me
as yours do
you

will it ever become
simple?
I suppose not

you are
teaching me
the meaning of
women's
friendship

Our Cats

when we first met
you said I was a nice lady
and then in quiet surprise
"You're a witch, too."

well, I don't know about
the words for what I am
but each of us has a
cat who's a familiar,
animal incarnation of ourselves.

for your cat struts around
making noises and mischief
demanding to be the center of attention
while mine fluffs her long fur, stretches,
and will sit on anybody's lap.

Winter Solstice I

In the depth of the season, darkness
Persephone far below
Tonight in her, a death of hope
Her cries to Mother Demeter stilled

The void rushes in – emptiness, darkness
Abysmal blackness yet containing all
Captive like the daughter
Emptiness to fill with death ... or light

Tonight, Persephone transmutes
The blackness to its coldest power
Purifying all dreams of past and future
Cleansing her underground paleness
With the earth in which she is entombed

Liberated from anticipation,
Freed now of all despair
Free of all anxiety and fear
Consecrated in darkness

Winter Solstice II

Donning our evergreen crowns
We greet the Dark Mother
Bowing before the bright spirit
For She is also Queen of the Sun
Dispersing the darkness
With pine to remind us of
The green and growing

For as She is Queen of earth and water
Also rules She air and fire
The growth of our harvest's greenness
Light-dappled forests where nymphs can play

The Queen of Darkness is now the
Queen of Light, Queen of the Stars,
Queen of the Moon, Lady of the Horn,
Queen of the Fires, Queen of the Earth

Reveal your presence as the
Sun comes up again
Blessed be the Great Mother!
Blessed Be!

Deadly Cigar

nuclear accident
nuclear refugees
in Pennsylvania
here I am in a demonstration again

a different war
the anti-nuclear resistance
coming over earthen bulwarks
from the first American revolution

seeing the deadly cigar
that can / will
destroy half the world
in twenty minutes

listening to strangely
déjà vu speeches –
humanistic health worker
paid one-quarter

her husband, father, brother
working on this death tool
called
Trident

somehow it would seem
more correct
to dance in circles, chant,
raise our energy

Fire

when the fire came back
I couldn't have been more surprised
gosh, I'd forgotten.

where's it been all this time?
how many years?
why am I angry?
is this any more guide to my living
          than any other feeling?

what a classic, I'm sitting in a car
just a kiss, a really fine one by the way
and your hand holds my shoulder
          arm around my neck behind.

and the fire comes back
licking up between my knees
my body's crying open
should you want to feel
its redder flames
          way up inside.

Long Wait

Though we've been together, you're not free
You'd never admit that
Most would say you're the freest one they know
Rebellious and untamed, brilliant

Others visit: a lanky painter
A student I drive home
More drama in a glance across your hedge
Than all of midnight's lick and plunge

I am always aware I want you
No one else will have my heart
Until we are together, all are friends,
A few share lavish play in the dark

Sitting Here in Love

sitting
next to you
aware of the spaces
between
yes
and
wait

the space between
my
thigh
and
yours

the spaces
between
our
ever
slower
words

Living Through Hurricanes

For a decade we live by the sea
Learning about each other
Learning to help one another
      Enjoying gardens
            driving kids around

I take your son to the skating rink
He gets good at it, travels to contests
I never learn just how to brake
      It hurts a lot
            when I fall down

My brother and his wife come visit
She teaches their son to call us "aunts"
In an old farmhouse with old windows
      We somehow survive
            two hurricanes

Hurricane Gloria and Hurricane Bob
Thrash the coastline uprooting trees
We huddle and hug behind the sofa
      Use candles, a camp stove
            with no power

In those years we grow stronger
Expand in new ways, learn new skills
You work much harder, earn your degree
      We gain strength
            then better jobs

In our hearts there are few questions
I know you are the one I want
You travel the world, come back to me
      There are no more
          inner storms

We both spend time to help our mothers
It's that time in daughters' lives
We take turns shopping and cooking
      Savor these more
          focused times

I am always more than grateful
To grow when you are growing too
We each gave up our "wild" and "angry"
      I don't miss them now
          – do you?

Family, After All

When the family, the father
Is now aging, in need
Those I respect care for their elders
So here I am in Illinois

I'm the daughter whose
Self-esteem was demolished
Insulted, rejected, refused
By then not tumbled far at all

You're cut off, he said
But allowed me the worth
Of jewels my grandmother
Once gave me, which he then kept

I'd married into the Ivy League
But the politics were wrong
Soon he called us traitors
I don't reveal when and why I leave

Once it's clear, Mom visits
Communes, a teepee home
Awkward, then better times
Respite for her with me, my friends

Yes, I helped, with a yard sale
Donations and a move
He's in day care, cannot drive
Now not certain of my name

Today no fury and no fire
Silence about the past
Perhaps our troubles signaled
Dementia's early path

His wild sister clucked over yet
Still admired, I tossed away
Who knows why? I learn this lesson:
Helping heals today

Charlie and the Fireflies

Timeworn collie in bare farmhouse
Watching neighbors, no sofa to stand on
Chin on windowsill, musing

Her family, two women
And the boy who grew and broadened this year
To be bigger than both

Tan station wagon comes back
Her people tired, breathless, sweat-smelling
Drive to a forest, smell squirrels

Old dog hears no waves, seagulls
Heeds instead robin, titmouse, Carolina wren
Her people give her water

Old dog by screen, breeze in fur
Begins to bark, her people slowly gather
One touches her back gently

Old dog sees glowing,
Twinkling lights, yellow-green, not in unison
Dozens in twilit back yard

Fireflies flash on - off - on
Seeking their mates in the night, a sight
Only a damp pond-side gives

All descend stairs to the yard,
Laughing, barking, sniffing, talking,
Smiling at fireflies – then, emerging stars

Parental Dissent

I got married when I had no idea for work
Back then, marriage a career
Dad said only marriage made lovemaking right
And only drunkards' wives needed jobs

Mom told me to look for
A conversation to last a life
Discussions with no rules or limits
She was the parent who got it right

Living in Nature

Ask yourself, do you see now
You are living in nature
Yes, the earth, the river, the trees
Water we drink, air we breathe

Ten years of water-testing
Of the mill pond where I live
Shows me these simple measures
Clarity, temperature, depth

And bacteria-levels tell
How Mother Nature does today
Heavy metal in the water
Shows how we have gone astray

I meet the mink, the raccoon, the turtles
Deer and otter, so many birds
Mating dragonflies divert me
Frightening fisher-cat brings fear

We are living in their nature
Remember, it's our nature too
If heron, kingfisher, osprey
Don't endure, we too will be doomed

Heart

That last day, she did not speak
She breathed roughly
Then she began to skip breaths

When breathing stopped
I put my ear to her heart
Felt it beat
… beat … skip … beat … and stop

Mom's heart at rest now, concerns gone
Are my children okay?
Partnered with good, true hearts?

Will war end?
Dorothy's cancer be stopped?
Grandson make his mark?

All quiet now
I told her friend that
She was gone

My origin, my first love
My mother
My source

The Best Things in Life are Still Free

The whistle of an osprey teaching her chicks to fish
The cool breeze that lifts my bangs off my forehead
The little dog who walks me twice a day
The biscuit that my neighbor gives her
All these are free.

An expression of kindness or understanding
A smiling, "Good morning!" in a market parking lot
The directions I give to the Community Garden
For an old woman offered surplus vegetables
All these are free.

Hugs when greeting and leaving friends
An honest answer to an awkward question
Replacing fear of war with a prayer for peace
Replacing criticism with encouragement
All these are free.

Trees whose shade makes my yard cooler
Your soft voice waking me for the day
Waves to neighbors as they leave for work
Thoughts of concern, hope, gratitude
All these are free.

Sonnet to My Love

Troubled, some said in the seventies,

Honky-tonking angel in your home town

Your strong, full voice witnessed love's agonies

Bright laughing eyes gave that life a thumbs down.

You have a sashaying walk as you come

To meet me, know me, and serenade me,

Working harder than anyone has done

As we blend our lives, gardens, families.

Night school, better jobs, lots of travel – good,

Now only I and your sons make you cry

You make songs, stained glass art, guitars of wood,

And gardens with small strong hands, we get by.

We hold hands to sleep, check in all day long,

When we marry, your vows are a sweet song.

Letting Go

Twelve-steppers say "Let Go and Let God"
If you try to manage a drinker or addict
Letting go is certainly key wisdom
The reverse of attachment – detachment
Periods of palpable serenity,
So different from the rest.

A man whose family suffered multi-generations
Of touching, betrayal by the same priest uncle
Is sixty-three when he tells me he is just starting
To take off his "anger coat"
Sitting across from me, he looks lighter, brighter,
Soon opens himself to love.

One day I stop crying in nursing home parking lots
As the sun strikes my face, my tense shoulders drop
It is not my decision, never will be:
My disabled goddaughter's feeding tube
She lives until the ninth year of her stroke,
And I have visited with calm.

I keep warning my young friends
Dancing, drinking, handsome boys in bars
When HIV-positive – affirm my love
Recall how, warned about LSD, I scoffed
Unlike my friends with AIDS so long ago,
They are strong – they are still here.

My own cancer struggle wakes me in my fifties
It is not "Why me?" but "Why not me?"
It leads me to different, more giving work
Teaching survivors helps me, too
For a life well-lived, we can ask,
How did you meet suffering?

There's a paradox there, key to survival
Detachment is a strength – healing it's true
Almost any hurt or pain now
Is best met with a lesson learned
If not today then soon suggests
Some work, some letting go, to do.

Circle of Life

I saw the hawk pair before the oaks leafed out,
Building a nest with twigs and branches
Seeming too weighty for their pigeon-sized bodies
Lining it with bark.

When the leaves came out it was harder to see,
I presumed the smaller was the female,
But learned she was the larger one
Sensible and strong.

They share our pond-side ecology for years,
He kills the small birds, she the larger
A quick flap long glide then, wings folded
Plummeting, they kill.

The eggs are dark streaked, one-third her size
She lays just one in two days
She incubates, defends against jays
He furnishes food.

Too small to straddle, he cannot sit on the eggs
Sharp talons a danger to the shells
He stays on the edge of the nest for her short hunts
Guarding against danger.

Four fledglings stand crying on the branch
While the hawks call them from further trees
Tawnier than their parents, a few days later
They flutter and call.

Fearless, they fly close by as they hunt
Near songbirds' nests, birdfeeders, bushes
Robin and sparrow parts, gold feathers
Strewn across the ground.

Six sharp-shinned hawks sweep the oak canopy
Whistling back and forth, scouting chase grounds
We fill our feeders and bird baths
Baiting their prey.

Halloween

Boundaries are thin
Between this world and the next
Children dress as if
They have climbed out of graves
Celts marked harvest's end
Start of the year's dark half.

Humankind celebrates dead loved ones
Cleans grave sites, prays for saints
And souls purgatory-stuck
Plants tombstones in yards
Makes sugar skulls
Proffers sweets.

We light a bonfire
Challenge the darkness
Friends, family hold
Warm hands around
Draw community
To endure winter's hardships

Listen closely for dispatches
From our ancestors
Sing names of two- and four-legged
Beloveds lost
Find awareness in
The proximity of final rest.

Veterans' Day

My little dog insists we walk
On this blustery and cold day
The wind rolls an American flag through puddles
As we come past an ancient beech tree
I pick up the flag with care

A broken staff at a gray house shows the owners
I roll the flag with utmost care
Walk up to the door and ring the bell
When no one comes I place it gently there
Plants, a porch chair shield it

As we walk, large C-40's fly so close overhead
Leaving, not coming to Quonset, maybe to train
Could they carry men, supplies to Syria
Or this a holiday demonstration despite the rain?
Some parades are called off

I saw a convoy Sunday steadily steering South
Dad served in the Navy against the Japanese
With school deferment, lucky lottery
His sons did not fight, killed no Vietnamese,
Suffer no Agent Orange dioxin cough

Yet we were all veterans of war
Mom's marriage strained by calls for war, for peace
A generation gap broad and deep
Estrangement, questioned loyalty, anger

Even those who loved unable
To hear each other's words, or know
Why veterans die homeless, soldiers are suicides,
What wartime did to Dad

Make A Difference: A-Z

Adopt a dog
Be authentic
Care for yourself
Discourage gossip

Express your love
Find a way
Grow food and flowers
Help someone

Introduce neighbors
Just smile
Kiss on meeting
Listen before you speak

Make lovely things
Never give up
Open your heart
Phone politicians

Question authority
Report abuse
Send birthday cards
Tell the truth

Understand another culture
Visit elders
Write poetry
eXamine racism

You are part of the solution
Zig-zag always toward peace

Solo Song for Kay Boyle

Like you I enjoyed privileged schooling
Learned from my mother to assist the poor
Marched for racial justice, women's rights, peace
Nor was I immune to loving's frequent lure.

A road winds up a mountain to a hideout
Like you, I find true peace in Mother Nature's signs
Hurricane winds can clear my mind and spirit
I gain strength from oak groves, paths through
fragrant pines.

Family far away, you lived poor in France
Your lover died of scarcity's disease, TB
Family far away, I danced through city nights
Friends perish from abandon's disease, HIV.

These things I have loved most of all in life
Quiet, birds, purple flowers on a fence, womankind
Their stories, my stories, truth no longer hidden
Layers of river mist give me peace of mind.

Paint Trees

Riding in the "quiet car" for the first time
Sounds: train on the tracks, whistle at crossings
Miles and miles of marshland and coastline.

Then a shock, auto graveyards
Scrap metal in piles
Slum housing, miles and miles of egotistical graffiti
Bright spray paint of your gang's name, your name
Mile upon mile upon mile.

Shocking, deeply embarrassing
How my country looks
Praying no Europeans are witnessing
Our lack of pride in our home
The trash, the names painted over names
To say, 'I did this," "I was here."

Saying it so much more poorly
Than sweeping the streets
Fencing the junkyards
Perhaps painting beautiful flowers
Painting trees.

Moon Dog

You lead once again
Outdoors after dark
I look up to see
If moon glows, stars shimmer

In the wintry chill
Half the sky clouded
With approaching snow
First high stars, then the moon

Cycle half complete
Show of reflected light
Above woman, small dog
Chill, constant sequence

What Changes?

What changes? As a young girl
I go with my Grandpa
A full day's drive to his downstate farm
In the small town, black families
Step off the sidewalk for us
Can't swim in the pool
Drown in the river.

What changes? Every week
A woman dark and round
Takes busses two hours from the South Side
To wash our floors on hands and knees
An adult not called "Mrs."
She is just "Inez"
She makes eight dollars.

What changes? A homegrown Nazi
George Lincoln Rockwell marches
Through Skokie, jolting its resettled Jews
And the ACLU defends
The bigots' right to march, speak
In film, Blues Brothers
Play the scene for laughs.

What changes? High school summer
Service in Chicago
An integrated group, a street fair
Fights break out, white boy is struck
Adults stop it, no real hurt
Yet monstrous anger
Brings me panic, tears.

What changes? In Charlottesville
Homegrown haters rally
Cornell West says his people would be
Crushed like cockroaches but whites
Stood between bigots and blacks
A white woman killed
Black man chased, bloodied.

What changes? Our motherland
Haunted by difference
Progressives blamed as much as haters
By the President – no one hears
Those who see diversity
Can make us stronger,
No one hears answers.

Patriarchy

For the teen who maltreated me at six
Touching countless children as a sitter
A special psychologist, help to lifelong job
Wife, children and grandchildren.

A small intact piece of tissue means
I get exam trauma but no special care
Doctor recommends no police report
"Just don't mention it to her."

Without that healing, I become shy
A boy I like walks me to the beach
He senses terror as he comes closer
Chooses to date another.

One's stepfather insists she touch him
Her mother accuses her of seduction
Blamed, thrown out, no more school
She is homeless at fifteen.

When another's mom has cancer, her dad
Says she must assume her every chore
After her foreseeable breakdown
Moves her in with a town whore.

Three bright girls with broken boundaries
Struggle with love, lead lacerated lives
I become a lonely, fearful freshman
Fondled by first man I kiss.

Fail marriage's first year, move thirty times
Before my 31st birthday, have no kids
Have no grandchildren
In age find fluency's force.

Decades later, one battles him in dreams
Screaming to this long-gone abuser that
He must die, her wrath
Awakens her, choking, sweat-soaked.

After hippie years, the third is
A weekend call girl, even though a nurse
Careless of her child
Grandchildren also damaged.

Three stories of several score shared
Many more to hear, yet we all are chastised –
It was our defect
Not a flaw allowed in men or boys.

Kingfisher

Your large head reminds me
Birds descended from dinosaurs
Proportioned to your body
Like that of Tyrannosaurus Rex

You live in a burrow
In the bank of our mill pond
But I haven't found it yet
Nor have I taken your picture

You move too fast, cackling
Laughing at me when I try
Too fast for me to look for
A female's blue stripe

Sometimes we are all head, too
Our thoughts and emotions rule
You need clear water to spear a fish
We clear minds to grasp life's gifts

United States 2018

When the gunman came in
She was just entering her classroom
Thinking she needed another coffee.

When the gunman came in
She was teasing another classmate
About a valentine he didn't send.

When the gunman came in
The Veterans' Home staff were meeting
About an elderly resident.

When the gunman came in
Families were ordering waffles
Relaxing together on Sunday.

When the gunman came in
Students were chatting at their lockers
Gangly teens moving between class.

When the gunman came in
Reporters were filing their stories
A few joking, most more serious.

When the gunman came in
She had just written "environment"
On the board and then, she turned around.

When the gunman came in
She was checking her grocery list
Wondering what she had forgotten.

When the gunman came in
She had begun to pray in Hebrew
For a soon-to-be named baby boy.

When the gunman came in
She felt improvement in her balance
Calmly held a tree pose, and she breathed.

When the gunman came in
She was tossing her hair and laughing
At learning the Texas two-step.

When the gunman came in
His doctor fiancée was working
Caring for the hurt, the sick, the pained.

Chair Yoga

So now we do our yoga
On and around chairs
A group of mature women
A couple of men

Our teacher Sarah avoids
Fancy yoga gear
For comfortable warm clothes
Hand-knit wool sweaters

Yes, we are silvery now
We have man-made knees
Ninety years' or cancer's aches
Reconstructed hips

Sarah's soft strong instructions
Lead us as we move
Spine-legs-feet-toes-arms-hands-head
Defer to limits

This is the most revealing
Practice that I do
And I am walking outdoors
Whenever I can

In this circle of wisdom
Excellent meditation
Quiet *savasana*
Beliefs most hopeful

Cold Moon

The night after Winter Solstice
A fifteen-hour full moon
Calls me to quiet self-care

Now, cease social concerns
So many years for racial justice,
Women's rights, an end to war

Stop nukes, find safe energy
Gay rights and clean water
Research for cancer cure

Raspberry and purple sunset
Striping the western sky
I return home, build a warming fire

Cuddle small dog under blankets
Tell you how I love you
Feel blessed for my many friends

Replace struggle, the movement
With privacy and quiet
A different time, prized and precious

Meteor showers the next night
Light up like my bone scans do
This quiet time will be for me, for you

Meeting My End

When cancer shows itself again, is it a surprise?
Last time I learned there were no sureties
To say, "Why not me?" instead of "Why me?"
Changed jobs to coach "survivors"
Grateful – they gave me courage
I taught them exercise
Raise some spirits, strengthen shortened lives.

As the year began, add work in a nursing home
Witness life's ending day after day
People make choices – to go, to live on
Such excellent care is not what I need
I've been told what will end me
I pray for some more time
My oncologist says I cannot be cured.

Last time I fought; believed I could be saved
My insurance company spent six figures
Doctors made me hideously ill
It was cancer, not me, they hoped to kill
Skull, legs, spine, sacrum, many more bones
Now cancer is extensive
Ask my doctor the years I "might" live.

Appointments, scans, injections
Disturb my balanced life
My financial guys revise my goals
Could this be fun? They include "Spend more!"
Eat chocolate, luxury trip to New Mexico
Pecuniary problems perish
No need to save to be ninety-five.

I weep. For ten years I have done all I can
To live now, yet leave some record I was here
When I share my news, people tell me they love me
I let them drive me when I could drive myself
For nightmares of crumbling bones
I could take a pill, or even three
But they wash away important dreams.

I pray the researchers will find a cure
Probably not for me, but for the ages
The powerful microscopes look
The researchers see what told cancer again to grow
The chemists invent a potion, hinder this message
Many survive for a time
But cancer will find a new trick of its own.

It is true that all will meet our end
Anger? Joy? Exhaustion? Fear?
After a life well-lived? Risks taken?
Rejoicing to at last meet God?
Am I grateful or sad my mother is gone?
That I did not have children?
Why, both of course, and so much more.

Early Spring

Tiny dog and I zig-zag up our street
Past old oaks standing dead
Killed by two years of caterpillars.

See snow necklaces under evergreens
Squill, snowdrops and crocus,
A few daffodils, brave planted pansies.

I am almost always tired now
My actions cut by half
Have an "If I do nothing else" list.

Writing class and Chair Yoga
Have fallen from the list
Poetry Group, one exercise class, stay.

If I do nothing else, these for fresh air:
Walking my dog, cleaning
Gardens – may flowers, not cancer, grow.

One day I subsist on peanut butter
Next vegetables, grains
Doesn't really matter what I eat or do.

If you ask how I am, first think: "So tired,"
But I may say, "Great!"
Doesn't really matter what I say is true.

Call to Rest

I love to walk with my dog under old trees
On streets and paths that curve
To meet with writers and poets
Enjoy sharp intelligence, varied lives
I have some poems written, others in my head.
Beyond all else, my recliner calls.

Brown microfiber designed to sit in rows
In a media room
No, it's not the height of fashion
Today, I could give a helpful talk on cancer,
Clean house, cook a meal, visit special friend.
Above all, my recliner calls.

I want to give friends and family a book
My body wages war
My yoga teacher says, "Peace, Peace,"
I want to cry, I am so tired, can't I
Rest for the rest of such a partial life?
Indeed, my recliner calls.

Can my imagined life be so docile
Have I nothing left to give?
Right now, just allow me to rest
Settle back, comfortable, eyes closed
My darling, just recognize I need to rest.
Now, my recliner calls.

The medications have been working a year
A temporary siege
I have no energy to dance,
Talk with you, read, color a mandala,
Let me sit, shell-shocked, struggle-stunned.
My recliner calls.

Backyard Summer

By September, the knotweed and jewel weed
Seem to be winning
The yard narrows and shortens as they advance.

The asters are all right; the array of dead plants,
Peonies, iris, lilies, bee balm gone by
Witness to my neglect.

As does a maple on the north side
Hidden by the wild grapevines
Who have made it their arbor.

Because I can do little, I note these and go on
Down to the quiet circle of oaks by the water
Sit on the cedar bench, fill up with peace.

Here, I will dump the pots I filled with soil
And never planted, now I will plant Virginia
Bluebells
Let the rest stay wild for now.

Four Haiku for Fall

I.

Goldenrod, asters
The sweet odor of wild grapes
Now Autumn is here.

II.

Bulb-planting begins
This year I plant white tulips
Happiness in Spring.

III.

This special Autumn
Dark moon after Equinox
Message of magic.

IV.

Approach second year
Daily gratitude improves
Living without cure.

Headstrong

Toes splayed, five-inch legs rotated out
Support sturdy head, neck, shoulders
Bets were made on 100 rats
Versus one Jack Russell in a ring.

Anxious pet, headstrong, twice adopted
You came to me just five years ago
A quirky, bossy little girl
You hate dogs, would never bite a child.

By morning you have all the covers
Stare at the sink, bark for fresh water
Slam the cabinet when hungry
Jump in my lap and huff to go out.

You put up with my constant talk
Perhaps you roll your eyes
Short legs walk miles on clear days
Make me strong, keep me alive.

A Place to Write

Because empty rooms in our house
Tend to fill with the stuff
We haven't time to put away
When we became empty-nesters
I made a bedroom into my office.

Bookcases, my late mother's desk,
Computer, printer, calendar,
Awards for river work are on the wall
Mom's role model Christine de Pizan,
In a frame from a Paris bookstall.

There's a shelf/altar in honor
Of my disabled god-daughter
Pictures, flowers, paper cranes
My Brain Injury Association badge
A tiny screaming ragdoll her mother sewed.

There are cartons of paper yet to sort
File drawers of journals yet to re-read
My grandmother's notes of the adventure
Taking her mother to Europe in 1933
The beginning of research for a family tree.

A Chinese fortune cookie informs me,
"Your home is a pleasant place
From which you will draw happiness."
This is very true, yet there will never be
A place for everything; everything in its place.

I need to work here more, perhaps winter's chill
Will bring me inside to read, sort, scan,
Enter as data, craft into stories, file, and shred
Recycle as paper or poetry, ship to my brothers
Clean up and clear up before I am dead.

Tiny Things

It's the phase of tiny things, seen for the first time,
DNA strands show us our common ancestor:
Small African woman, dark and strong
Faint light of ancient stars, seen for the first time,
As Hubble scientists calculate, then see
When, where, how this universe began.

A microscopic enzyme, seen for the first time,
Living near another tiny thing:
A cancer cell that eluded treatment for a decade
Ordering voids in bone, seen for the first time,
In my happiest, most delight-filled year
Doctors cannot tell when my universe will end.

I've always thought my soul was starshine,
Surrounded by coolness and space
Living in my body for its short time on earth
Bright when I laughed on a swing at five
Or when I helped a troubled friend
A tiny spark in my worst times, then huge
Limitless and bright, dancing the universe again.

Aging Brain

Is it chemo brain?
My cancer counselor calls it stress
It could also be my attempts
In my twenties for lysergic spirituality
Or my dad's Alzheimer's.

I can't use numbers
This week I almost give a waiter
A triple tip ... search
Hours for wrong address
Lose a necessary bottle of pills
Some place or another.

I disremember
How to reinstall my bifold door
I overcook simple meals
For my patient love
Leave my hair dryer running red hot
Could have burned down our home.

But these I can do:
Follow my dog on three-mile ramble
She has learned so well
Put my hands together
In prayer at police or ambulance
Stopped at a neighbor's home.

Perhaps fresh air makes
Me smarter ... walks, trips to the woodpile
Sitting on the front steps
Watching for the hawks
Raking weeds, moving plants, tending blooms
Listening to birdsong.

Tuesday Haiku

I.

Three vultures glide above
As I walk to the mill pond
Silent reminder.

II.

Gardening morning
Gloves damp inside, muddy knees
Plants fed, bed aglow.

III.

Noon Reiki session
Healing hands encompass me
Clarity ousts dread.

IV.

Poetry group meets
Own poems, favorite poems shared
Cordial word lovers.

Fatigue

Is it cancer or the pills
That check its growth
Doesn't really matter now
I do short bursts of housework
Followed by rest
Rest day before special events
And day after.

Too dull to read a story
In *New Yorker*
By favorite Zadie Smith
Finding energy later
To savor her
Channeling of Lady Day
Finally can.

Acceptance makes me search for
Strength to struggle
While faintness is more frequent
Than the pain in punctured bones
I can prevail
Rest restores physical power
I persevere.

Walking

Her leg broke and she fell
Carrying groceries up her stairs
Sat there a long time, so much pain
Gone in two short years
Now just in her family's prayers

Now I always carry a phone
Just in case I break and fall
Yet some days I walk for miles
Take in fresh air
Smile, look, laugh, enjoy it all

Days I do this demand a nap
Soft bed, thick covers shielding light
The day's work accomplished:
Motion, air, thoughts I savor
Silence, smiles, sights

Santa Fe Sojourn

Air smelling of pinon pine
Gold leaves falling from cottonwood trees
Rounded adobe buildings like women's tan bodies
My first visit to Santa Fe.

Museums of folk art and native works
Lectures on history, healing, O'Keeffe
Cooking lessons for a Southwestern meal
Salsa so hot I cannot eat.

Zen Center at the top of a hill
Silent meditation, walking meditation
Breakfast conversation with women witty and wise
Seeking learning, respite from complex lives.

Hot springs: iron for blood and digestion
Next soda for immunity, roofed against the sun
Lithium for mood the one I sense at once
In arsenic for arthritis I clench, unclench my hands.

Ghost Ranch once The Valley of the Witches
When cattle thieves hoped to keep others away
I walk a desert labyrinth singing "All Will Be Well"
Finishing, my arms lift like wings to the sky.

High Desert Healing

Small, short and dark
Patricia calls in the directions
Smudges with sage smoke
Her apprentice wafts with an eagle feather
Blesses our visit.

We meet mid-week
Lovely, brightly-clad Nickie weeps and tells
Of her brother's death
In her arms — now she senses how grateful
He truly was.

I wait till the end
To say, "I came because of you,
My cancer is advanced
To extensive bone metastases,"
She touches me.

"No, you are well."
And uncertainty evaporates
Right now, this moment
Cancer is static, not growing, not deadly
No source for concern.

The last day, we
Circle around a hint of altar
Sketched with fallen leaves
Each gets a guardian angel medal
I, a dragonfly.

Crystals glittering
It brings lightness, joy, transformation
Hopeful freedom from fear
My beliefs free of pain, Patricia says,
"You are a warrior."

For peace, grace, joy
And creativity – Patricia makes
Magic beaded bags
I fight for insurance approvals
And make some poetry.

Generations
Were midwives, healers, counselors
Comforters at death
Whether on the pueblos or in Santa Fe
Or now, on The Web.

Sharing sorely
Needed comfort, medical intuitive
Acupuncturist
You have great power in your small stance
And the world changes.

We are coming
From the darkness into a brighter light
New species appear
Heavy metals evaporate more quickly
Bees fly in January.

Magnetic fields shift
Earth is in a new part of her galaxy
Birds must adapt
Weather changes, earth's axis also
Women take control.

Oak Moon

I view the moon
Though high oak branches
Her cycle, her gravity's pull
Change my mood, my sleep
My immunity

The oaks have their own magic
A magic of strength and power
Sacred to the moon in summer
I can hug an oak for advice
Like a druid

Medicines the doctors give me
Follow the moon's cycle
Waxing/waning over twenty-eight days
Slowing cancer (unable to end it)
Oak, protect me

Spell for living with cancer:
When the moon is new
State intentions – a good season,
Love, friends, music, art, kind acts
Reverse all fear

When she is full, express thanks
That hopes were achieved
The acorn in your pocket kept illness away
Through the dark of the moon – rest
Begin again

My Name

'Devine' was from Dad
And my middle name 'Frances'
Though he spelled his with an 'i'
Both of us for the Saint of Assisi
As was his mother, 'Mary Frances Ryan.'

In Ireland 'Devine' was another name, now lost,
Changed in New Haven when John, 16,
Got off the boat
He went to a West Virginia bridge-building uncle
Our line descended with that name.

'Dorothy' for my mother's distinguished aunt,
An early female medical doctor
She delivered babies at Chicago Lying-In
Dorothy was surely a lesbian,
Her beloved partner's name lost
When my mother died fourteen years ago.

Thus, Dorothy Devine, a name
That could read 'gift of God divine'
Perhaps should have been a pastor or spiritualist,
Dressed all in white
Or I should be an actress, dancer, stripper
Artists' model the closest I came

Because my diagnosis bridges
'Chronic' and 'terminal,' I find
I contemplate spirit most and wonder
What of me might stay on, shine?

Sisters (For Valerie)

In the war of my youth
Brothers in arms killed to avenge
The brothers lost on patrol
Not for tin mines or political goals.

Danger-forged bonds
Visions of maiming, pain, and death
Continuing through old age
Jobs, marriages, parenting outweighed.

My sisters in arms
We hear of endless cancer deaths
We are cut, poisoned, and burned
Treasure those who likewise learned.

Still standing, strength in grace
Exhausted, hoping for a cure
Helpless to prevent or ease
Hear time and again of casualties.

Still visit hospitals
Like soldiers, feel survivors' guilt
Still spared as sisters die
Read obituaries, send tributes, cry.

Dread

Dread, terrible word, mood I hate
Makes me cry more as years pass
Raising my blood pressure
Shouldering aside delight

Try to live in today, harder done than said
More and more as more years pass
The Cancer Center sets me off
Want to turn and run, but where?

Full of apprehension I visit
The ever-cheerful receptionists
Smart, sensible social worker
Pretty doctor, nurses tired and kind

It's crazy but even being told
Cancer is stable can make me weep
I organize life around these visits
Lose track of what I must complete

This sickness doesn't feel systemic
It's mostly in the emotional sphere
Bone pain managed for the moment
But what if I fall when you're not here?

Passing Friends

When we make friends in Cancerland
We share indecision, immobility
Learn of success, marriages, children
In obituaries.

We rage at doctors, hospitals
Remember dates of one another's tests
Say "You do not have to tell me"
Diffuse each other's stress.

Retired while sick young mothers work
Limping into age as younger friends die
Writing poems as their artistry ends
Feeling guilty to survive.

Too many medical stories
Our families no longer want to hear
The 23rd Psalm in my pocket
Divides healing from a cure.

We share what may be unfinished
Who will get relics of ancestors, our jewels?
Who will care for my dog, your cats, the kids?
Who must we excuse?

Will my love drink away the pain?
Will your family falter when you're gone?
We go to sign another guest book
Mourn again, move on.

Questions

These new drugs can be confusing
No one knows how long they'll work
Of others I know with this illness
Four perished just this year
Is feeling sorry for myself a waste?
How am I supposed to feel?
Should I tell my love again I love her
Just so she'll be sure?

Timer-prompt a dozen pills
Eyedrops, special mouthwash too
I go to a clinic for injections
Choose immune-boosting food
Health appointments every week
Physical therapy, scans and tests
One medicine attacks my teeth
Aches and fear attack my rest

Should I write my obituary?
Plan a celebration of my life?
All the rest has been arranged
Uncertainty the ruler of these times
Will I soon become much sicker?
And how will that begin?
In the past just one in five survived
Through this crucial year, the fifth

Three skeletal events once the edge
How much more can this hurt?
Ribs, shoulder, hip, and leg my four now
Is this limit still correct?
If disease progresses from my bones
It means this treatment failed
Will I try another remedy?
Or refuse it due to age?

Of course, there are pills for mood
Psychiatrist, counselor, cancer group
Some with metastasis splurge on travel
All live for today
I meet with my young minister
Once just sit and cry
He thinks I must be feeling worse
Yet much is just the same

These new drugs can be confusing
Should I pretend I'm well?
Cancer extensive, growing slow now
How can I complain?
I've lived longer than expected
Feel tired and achy more than ill
Strive to be grateful as life lingers
Detest my worry-weakened will

Waiting for Science

We're on the brink of a cancer cure
Or, "durable remission"
More kinds now can be remedied
Possibly not mine
Life is good, I have advanced
From fragility and fearful flight
From someone who was injured
        To someone who
            could help

My ideals remained constant
I never flirted with a cult
Never had to be "born again"
Erasing ghastly guilt
I rejoined the family of my birth
Left behind so long ago
Helped as daughters are meant to help
        Saw my own part
           in the gulf

Of course, I hurt others and was hurt
In the search for love and home
But once I learned to love myself
Love bloomed and grew right here
I know I fear the dying piece
Perhaps confusion, especially pain
Hurting those I love with loss
        Choosing, "No more treatment"
          seems a suicide

How to Be a Lifelong Friend (For Janet)

When your friend returns from travel, visit
If she is single, invite her for Christmas Eve
Wedding, christening, funeral – invite your friend
If you marry, ask her to be your matron of honor.

Make your childless friend your kids' godmother
Make grandchildren you raise her godchildren too
Someone to love and encourage, dreams to know
To help with college books and child care fees.

Listen to every awkward thing she has done
Try to top it with a distressing one of your own
Share when, why you are mourning or rejoicing
Together, you can cry, you can laugh.

Living far apart, include her in family reunions
Meet halfway for lunch every few months
When you get older, have more of these lunches
Hire a driver if you must, make sure to get there.

To be a lifelong friend, teach her to be one, too
Share with others how to do this, how precious
Until whatever life's triumphs, torments, turns
None need feel afraid, cut off, alone.

Sea of Friends

Community, what we need
Coupled, widowed or alone
This will help each survive

For so many years alone
Or with a mistaken one
I now stretch, smile, feel alive

Swimming in a sea of friends
Kind hearts, witches, writers, moms
Artists and poets, the circle grows

Minister, classmates, neighbors
River stewards, bike trail planners
Helpers, health and fitness trainers

Lesbians for decades joined
Towering guys with gentle ways
Tale-filled widows, durable and deep

Rides to doctors if you're sick
Bringing soup or birthday cake
Folks whose dogs my dog berates

Walking partners, yoga class
Librarians, local bands
Once forlorn, my life expands

What's to Come

Love and clarity will remain
When my body goes to ash
Dreams of white light surround me
Energy loftier than love.

I gently practice directing
This wisdom to regrets, remorse,
Difficulties dull in memory – depart
I grow brighter nearing death.

I realize I will rejoice
Even bodiless and gone
Shining light back to the troubled
Sending something better home.

When I Die

When I die, I want my flowerbeds free of crab grass

My sweet love putting herself before others

Our furniture re-upholstered and bright

Ten more years to get it right

Acknowledgements

Patchwork would not exist without the
encouragement and support of
the Neighborhood Guild Creative Writers
and the Willett Free Library Poets Group.

I am especially grateful to my first reader,
A. Littlestone,
and to
Linda Langlois,
who believed in me.

Made in the USA
Middletown, DE
24 April 2019